Cop

All rights reserved

The characters and events portrayed in this book are fictitious. Any similarity to real persons, living or dead, is coincidental and not intended by the author.

No part of this book may be reproduced, or stored in a retrieval system, or transmitted in any form or by any means, electronic, mechanical, photocopying, recording, or otherwise, without express written permission of the publisher.

First paperback edition June 2023

Book Jacket Design by Jessica Smith

ISBN Number (Paperback)
979-8-218-23050-0

In all things, I desire to bring glory to Jesus, my Savior, and my Redeemer. Without Him, I am nothing. In Him, all things are possible!

For Eric, Leo, & Chloe- my greatest blessings.

PRACTICAL AMERICAN ENGLISH

Learn English Through Conversations & Stories

Jessica Smith

INTRODUCTION

Learning a second language is a gift that will only enhance and prosper you and your life.

Therefore, learning a language should never feel heavy or overbearing. It should in many ways feel like a dance. Exciting, yet slightly intimidating, unexpected, challenging at times, and always rewarding.

In this book, we will learn English by exploring native everyday English as it's spoken in the USA. Everyday American English is so *chalk full of* idioms and slang, that for many, it feels completely foreign in comparison to academic English.

Where does this leave you? You might feel confused or even lost when listening to natives speak. Whether you have studied academic English for just a few months, or even a few years, you probably feel a bit blindsided and frustrated by all of this.

In this book, Practical American English, you will discover the essential idiomatic expressions, modern vocabulary, and slang necessary to understand real everyday English.

I hope you will enjoy the gift of learning English, and that you will trust the process as you enrich your understanding. Welcome to the dance!

CONTENTS

Copyright

Dedication

Title Page

Introduction...4

Expressions...5

To Hang Tight..6

To Make Do...8

To Butt In...10

To Lose One's Train of Thought...12

To Kick Oneself..14

To Scarf Down...16

To Bail...18

To Keep One's Eyes Peeled..20

To Wing It..22

To Be Good To Go..24

To Feast One's Eyes On..26

To Scoot Over..28

To Stir The Pot..30

To Divvy Something Up..32

To Be A Tough Call..34

To Be Floored..36

To Grow on Someone...38

To Milk It...40

To Take a Crack At It...42

To Ruffle Someone's Feathers....................................44

To Table It...46

To Be A Dud..48

To Throw In The Towel..50

To Shoot The Breeze...52

To Call It A Day...54

To Nail It...56

To Keep Someone Posted..58

Stories...61

Mr. Green & Ms. Ruddy..62

Sleep..65

Out For the Evening...69

Happily Married..73

Friends..77

The Visit..81

Blue Bridges..85

Milo & Max..89

About The Author...93

EXPRESSIONS

TO HANG TIGHT

DEFINITION: TO WAIT WITH SOME TENSION FOR A SOLUTION OR FURTHER INSTRUCTIONS.

Dad To The Rescue.

>Dad: Hello?
>Jane: Dad! I need some help.
>Dad: What's wrong honey? Are you ok?
>Jane: Yeah I'm ok now, but my tire just blew in the middle of the freeway. I'm in shock, but I'm ok. I'm on the side of the road, and I don't know what to do. Can you come please?
>Dad: Of course, I'll be right there with the spare, and my tools. **Hang tight** and put your blinkers on.
>Jane: Ok, thanks so such Dad!

Jane must wait until her dad arrives to fix her flat tire for her.

VOCABULARY

- *The spare:* the extra tire.
- *Honey:* a loving term of endearment for family members or close friends; similar terms include *dear* and *sweetheart*.
- *Blinkers:* flashing lights or turn signals in a car.

EXTRA EXAMPLES

- Just **hang tight** until Monday, and then we will decide.
- You'll have to **hang tight** until I get home.
- Don't make a rash decision, just **hang tight** until the meeting.

PRACTICAL AMERICAN ENGLISH

At The Airport.

>Attendant: Hello sir, how may I assist you today?
>Mr. Fox: Yes, my flight to Miami was canceled this morning, and I want to check to see if it has been rescheduled yet?
>Airline Attendant: Alright, Mr. Fox, let me check on that.
>Mr. Fox: Thank you.
>Airline Attendant: Ok, I'm seeing here that the flight was canceled due to impending weather conditions. Unfortunately, this means that we are unable to give you an updated itinerary at this time since the weather is out of our control. We need you to **hang tight** until further notice.
>Mr. Fox: Can you at least provide me with a voucher for a hotel since its getting late?

Mr. Fox must wait until the dangerous weather passes in order for the airlines to reschedule his flight.

VOCABULARY & EXTRA EXAMPLES

• *Impending weather:* terrible weather that will occur soon.

• *Itinerary:* a planned route.

• *Voucher:* a ticket that can be used instead of money to pay for something.

ADDITIONAL AIRPORT VOCABULARY

• *To board:* to get onto the plane.

• *Boarding pass:* plane ticket.

• *To book a flight:* to pay for a flight.

• *Carry-on luggage:* luggage that stays with you in flight.

TO MAKE DO

DEFINITION: TO MANAGE WITH WHAT IS ALREADY AVAILABLE.

Soup.

>Mom: It is so frigid outside today! Why don't we make Grandma's chicken noodle soup for lunch?
>Aunt Jo: Oh that's a great idea! I've been jonesing for that all week actually! How did you know?
>Mom: I really had no idea! It just sounds so good! I think we have everything, except, the recipe calls for yellow onions, and wide egg noodles. I'm not sure we have either of those.
>Aunt Jo: Well, lets just **make do** with what we have. We can swap the yellow onions for these leeks, and I have some regular egg noodles. They aren't wide, but they'll do.
>Mom: I hope the kids will eat it. They are so picky sometimes!

Mom and Aunt Jo don't have all of the ingredients for the recipe, so they will make the necessary substitutions.

VOCABULARY

- *Frigid:* very cold.
- *Jonesing for something:* to crave something.
- *Calls for:* requires.
- *Swap:* to substitute.
- *They'll do:* they are an acceptable substitution.
- *To be picky:* to be very particular about one's choices; fussy; difficult to please.

Pink Cabinets.

\>Roxie: We really need to update our kitchen.
\>Stan: What are you talking about?
\>Roxie: Our kitchen, Stan! It is so outdated. Let's take out a loan and do some renovations. I mean, look at the backsplash. It's pink. Don't get me started on the popcorn ceiling.
\>Stan: I know its old, but can't we just **make do**? I'd hate to have to take out a loan.
\>Roxie: I know, it's technically still functional, but these pink cabinets, are such an eyesore. I really think we should at least consider it. I'd love to have a huge island with new countertops. Come on Stan, please??
\>Stan: I guess I can look into it.

Stan and Roxie's kitchen is old, and outdated. Roxie really wants to renovate it, but since it is still functional, Stan would rather just keep the kitchen as it is.

VOCABULARY

• *Outdated:* out of style.

• *Renovations:* home updates.

• *Backsplash:* tiled areas between cabinets and countertops to protect the wall from damage or grime.

• *Don't get me started on:* used to avoid a topic which one has strong feelings about.

• *Popcorn ceiling:* stipple ceiling; ceiling with a bumpy texture.

• An eyesore: something that is ugly.

• *A kitchen island:* a freestanding piece of cabinetry with countertops in the middle of a kitchen.

- *Look into it:* to investigate something.

TO BUTT IN

DEFINITION: TO INTERRUPT, INTRUDE, OR INTERFERE.

Gossip.

>Jerry: I heard that he was fired from his last job.
> Andy: Yeah, I heard that too. I also heard that he lied about being sick, and missing work yesterday.
>Jerry: Yeah, I bet he just overslept. He seems so lazy to me. He moves so slowly and just mopes around. Whenever I try to strike up a conversation with him, it's miserable. It's like pulling teeth trying to get him to say anything!
> Sarah: Hey guys, I'm not trying to **butt in**, but I just think you should know that Andy wasn't at work yesterday because his grandfather passed away.

Jerry and Andy are gossiping about their coworker. Sarah hears their conversation, and interrupts to reveal truth to her coworkers.

VOCABULARY

- *To oversleep:* to sleep past one's alarm.
- *To mope:* to act dejected and unhappy.
- *To pass away:* to die.
- *To strike up a conversation:* to initiate a conversation.
- *Like pulling teeth:* extremely difficult to do.

USAGE

This expression is very informal. It is negative, and means to offer suggestions, when they are not welcome. Most people do not want to be interrupted while speaking. It's only acceptable to butt in if it is extremely important, or absolutely necessary to do so.

Mind Your Business.

>Sarah: Barb is driving me crazy. She's always **butting in** with suggestions for putting my baby to sleep.
> Jane: Oh no, really? You don't even know her that well. I hate it when people meddle.
>Sarah: Exactly! I've tried to tell her that we are fine, but she never gets the hint! She just keeps giving me her two cents.
> Jane: I'm sorry! I hope she will get the hint, and that she can be more supportive of you.
>Sarah: If it happens again, I'm probably going to tell her to mind her own business!

Sarah is complaining that Barb is always butting in with suggestions when Sarah only wants her to listen. Jane is a supportive friend who is showing compassion to Sarah.

VOCABULARY

- *To meddle:* to interfere in matters that don't concern you. *It is more intense and intrusive than butting in.*
- *To get the hint:* to understand someone's indirect suggestion.
- *To offer one's two cents:* to express one's opinion.
- *Mind your own business:* a rude way to tell someone to stop interfering in matters that don't concern them.

POLITE WAYS TO INTERRUPT:

- *Excuse me....*
- *I don't mean to interrupt, but...*

- *Do you mind if I jump in and add something?*
- *Can I mention something?*
- *May I interrupt for a second?*
- *Could I say something?*

TO LOSE ONE'S TRAIN OF THOUGHT

DEFINITION: TO FORGET WHAT ONE WAS THINKING OR TALKING ABOUT.

What Was I Saying?

>Stan: So, I was talking to Greg yesterday... Oh wow! Did you hear that thunder??
>Wilma: Oh yeah. Looks like it's pouring down rain outside!
>Stan: I had no idea it was supposed to rain today! Now, what was I saying? I **lost my train of thought**.
> Wilma: You were telling me about your conversation with Greg yesterday. What did he say?

*Stan wants to tell Wilma about his conversation with Greg. He is distracted by the sudden thunder and **looses his train of thought** until Wilma reminds him.*

VOCABULARY

- *Pouring down rain:* refers to a heavy rain.

MORE WAYS TO SAY "TO LOSE YOUR TRAIN OF THOUGHT":
- *I meant to invite her, but it completely **slipped my mind**.*
- *He practiced all day for his speech, but when it was time, his **mind** just **went blank**!*
- *I had **a senior moment**, and I completely forgot the name of our

neighborhood!

New York.

>Zoe: Hey Rose, congrats on your promotion! What does your family think about you transferring all the way to the New York office?
>Rose: Thanks Zoe, I actually haven't had a chance to tell them yet. I was trying to tell my mom about it today, but the kids kept interrupting me while I was on the phone with her.
>Zoe: Ugh, I hate it when that happens.
>Rose: Right?! Bella kept yanking on my shirt, and Henry was yelling that he needed help from upstairs. I couldn't even finish a sentence. **I lost my train of thought** so many times, that I just gave up, and told my mom I'd call her later.
>Zoe: Oh, I totally get it. My kids do it too! What are ya gonna do?? Well, anyways, congrats! You deserve it! And good luck telling your family!

Zoe asks Rose about her family's reaction to her move to New York. Beth relays that she hasn't been able to tell her family yet. She tried to call to tell her mom, but was interrupted so many times, that she kept forgetting what she was saying - **loosing her train of thought.**

VOCABULARY & EXTRA EXAMPLES

• *To yank:* to pull aggressively or forcefully.

• *I totally get it:* I completely understand.

• *What are ya gonna do:* an expression that emphasizes the fact that there isn't really a solution.

TO KICK ONESELF

DEFINITION: TO BLAME OR CRITICIZE ONESELF FOR SOMETHING.

Office Regrets.

<Anna: Hey! Did you see that Jan's company is taking all of the employees on a cruise this summer? That is amazing!
<Emma: I know! So amazing. I'm definitely **kicking myself** for not joining her company last year when I had the chance.
<Anna: They offered you a job?
<Emma: Yes! However, at the time I wasn't sure I could swing the work load. Now I really regret not taking a chance on it.
<Anna: Don't worry about it! I'm sure another opportunity will come along.

Emma regrets not taking a job, because the company is proving to be very successful.

VOCABULARY & EXTRA EXAMPLES

- *To swing something:* to manage or arrange something.
- *Work load:* work responsibilities.

MORE WAYS TO EXPRESS REGRET.

- *I should have/ shouldn't have...*
- *If only I had...*
- *If I could do it all over again, I would...*
- *I wish I had.....*

Engaged.

<Tyler: Oh man, did you hear that Elizabeth got engaged?
<Evan: She did? I'm really **kicking myself** for not asking her out when I had a chance in college. She's got the whole package.
<Tyler: Yeah, she's pretty great. What were you thinking??
<Even: Hey, she's not hitched yet! I might still go for it!

Tyler regrets not taking the opportunity to date Elizabeth in the past when he could have.

VOCABULARY & EXTRA EXAMPLES

- *Whole package:* someone who possesses everything desirable for a romantic partner.
- *To be hitched:* to be married.
- *To go for it:* to try to obtain something.

MORE EXPRESSIONS WITH KICK:

- *Kickin' it*: to relax and be with friends.
- *To kick the bucket*: to die.
- *To kick back*: to relax.
- *To get a kick out of something*: to enjoy something or to find something fun.
- *To kick something*: to stop a bad habit.
- *To kick something around*: to discuss it informally.
- *To kick someone out*: to expel by force.

TO SCARF DOWN

DEFINITION: TO EAT SOMETHING QUICKLY.

Lunch.

<Elaine: Thanks for meeting me for lunch George!
<George: Sure thing. Thanks for the invite!
<Elaine: You're welcome. We just **scarfed down** so much food!
<George: I know. We were starving!
<Elaine: Yes! Totally! We also only had 20 minutes for lunch, so it's a good thing we **scarfed** it **down**.
<George: Yeah, the company really needs to extend our lunch break, 20 minutes is not enough.
<Elaine: I absolutely agree!

Elaine and George quickly eat their lunches because they were starving and their lunch break was too short.

VOCABULARY & EXTRA EXAMPLES

- *Sure thing:* slang for *of course!*
- *It's a good thing:* used to show thankfulness for something that has happened.

WAYS TO SAY "DRINK QUICKLY"

- She was so hot that she quickly **guzzled** down her water.
- It was nasty, but he **downed** all of the medicine.
- They **chugged down** all of the lemonade before even eating!

We Gotta Go!

\<Abby: You had better **scarf down** that bagel because we have to leave in 5 minutes!
\<Madison: 5 minutes??
\<Abby: Yes, we can't be late. Hurry up and eat so we can get out the door!
\<Madison: Ok, I'm hurrying!

Abby urges Madison to hurry and finish her bagel so they can leave and not be late.

TIME EXPRESSIONS

- *To spread like wildfire*: to spread very quickly.
- *In the nick of time:* only just in time.
- *At the drop of a hat:* immediately without delay.
- *Time is money:* one's time is as valuable as one's money.
- *When the time is ripe:* when the conditions are good, and the moment has come.

Gabby was embarrassed because the news of her failing grade had *spread like wildfire* throughout the school. She texted Mom, who offered to pick her up *at the drop of a hat*. Mom also reminded Gabby that when the *time was ripe*, she would pass her exam. Her mom was right, *just in the nick of time*, Gabby passed. She was elated to begin her journey at college, while continuing to work part time. Gabby hoped to graduate college early. She was a hard worker, always using her time wisely, remembering, *time is money*.

TO BAIL

DEFINITION: TO SUDDENLY ABANDON A PERSON.

Golf Buddies.

<Frank: Hey man! How's it going?
<Tim: Hey buddy! All's good. Happy to get out here and swing the club around a bit.
<Frank: Don't I know it!
<Tim: Is Brad here yet?
<Frank: No, I don't think so. I haven't seen him.
<Tim: You don't think he **bailed on** us do you?
<Frank: Brad? Nah. He loves golf more than I do! No way he'd miss playing, especially on a day as nice as today. Oh there he is! Hey there champ!
>Brad: Hey fellas! Sorry I'm late. I had to take our dog Max to the vet. Ya'll ready to play?

Frank and Tim are waiting at the golf course for their friend Brad to arrive. Tim thinks it's possible that Brad ignored their plans to play golf and won't show.

VOCABULARY & EXTRA EXAMPLES

- *Swing the club around*: slang for *playing golf*.
- *Don't I know it*: I agree.
- *Nah*: slang for no.
- *Champ/ fellas*: slang for male friends.
- *Y'all*: you both or all of you (plural); *mostly used in the

southern parts of the USA.

You'll Never Guess.

<Daisy: Hey Mary, it's me Daisy.
<Mary: Hey friend!
<Daisy: You'll never guess what happened.
<Mary: What???
<Daisy: Well, you know how Kate and I were supposed to meet for coffee today?
<Mary: Yeah?
<Daisy: She **bailed on** me! Can you believe it? I went ahead and ordered my coffee, and sat down to wait for her. Finally, about an hour later, after I had already given up, she texted me to say she couldn't make it!
<Mary: Oh no! Did she say why??
<Daisy: No! That's the worst part, she didn't even apologize! I'm never making plans with her again.
<Mary: I don't blame you! I'm sorry that happened to you!

Daisy calls her friend Mary to tell her that her other friend Kate didn't come for coffee as they planned.

VOCABULARY & EXTRA EXAMPLES

• *I don't blame you:* an expression used to confirm that an action or thought is thought to be reasonable or correct.

MORE WAYS TO SAY SOMEONE BAILED:

• We planned to meet at the library, but he was ***a no show***.
• He asked me on a date last Friday, but he **stood** me **up**. I ate dinner and dessert all alone.
• My tire burst on the highway, and he was supposed to come and help,

*but he didn't! He **left** me **stranded** until I finally called my sister for help.*

❖ ❖ ❖

TO KEEP ONE'S EYES PEELED

DEFINITION: TO BE ALERT OR READY FOR SOMETHING.

Exit 12.

<Sam: How do I get to your house from the store?
<Mike: It's easy. Just hop onto I-95 east, and **keep your eyes peeled** for exit 12 on the right. I think its McGreggor's street.
<Sam: Ok. It sounds easy enough. I'll call you if I get lost!
<Mike: Alright, no worries. I'll see you in a bit.

Sam isn't sure how to get to Mike's house from the store. He tells her how to get there and advises her to be alert in order to not miss the exit.

VOCABULARY & EXTRA EXAMPLES

- *I-95*: "I" is the abbreviation for interstate.
- *To hop on*: To quickly get onto or join something- the internet, a road, a bus, a plane, a bike, a train, a phone call.
  - John, can you **hop on** the video conference with me?
  - He had the car, so I **hopped on** the bus to get downtown.
  - She **hopped on** the plane and was home within a few hours.

SIMILAR EXPRESSIONS TO KEEP YOUR EYES PEELED:

- **Be on the lookout** for more of that coffee!
- Make sure to **keep an eye out** for your brother. He should be here within the hour.

• *You need to **pay attention** so that you don't get hurt.*

The Zoo.

\<Tess: I'm so glad we finally made it to the zoo!
\<Sasha: I know, me too!
\<Tess: What do you want to see first?
\<Sasha: Well, you know I love the polar bears, but my other friend Lilly has been raving about the Rainforest Exhibit!
\<Tess: Oh yeah! I saw a commercial for that!
\<Sasha: Yes! Lilly said that as you walk through the exhibit, it feels like you are actually in a rainforest! Lilly said to **keep our eyes peeled** for the tree frogs and the butterflies.
\<Tess: Aw, I love butterflies! Ok, I say let's go there first.
\<Sasha: Do you have the map handy?
\<Tess: Let me see, I stuck it in my purse. Yes, here it is.
\<Sasha: Great. Ok it looks like we need to head towards the Brazil Exibit because the Rainforest Exhibit is right across from it.
\<Tess: Let's go!

Tess and Sasha are visiting the zoo. Sasha's friend Lilly encouraged her to visit the Rainforest Exhibit. She advised Sasha to lookout for the tree frogs and butterflies.

VOCABULARY & EXTRA EXAMPLES

• *To rave about something:* to praise something or someone.
• *To be handy:* to be convenient, useful, or close in proximity.
• *Let me see:* one needs a moment to think or consider something.
• *To stick something somewhere:* to put something in a specific place.
• *To head towards:* to go in that direction.

TO WING IT

DEFINITION: TO DO SOMETHING WITHOUT PREPARATION.

Test Time.

<Shawn: Yo man, are you ready for this test?
<Chris: No dude. I am **winging it**. I've been so busy with basketball practice and work, I haven't had a chance to study this week at all.
<Shawn: Oh no man. That sucks. Good luck bro.
<Sasha: Thanks man, Imma need it.

Two college friends Chris and Sam, are about to take a test. Chris hasn't prepared for the test, and is just doing the best he can without having studied.

VOCABULARY & EXTRA EXAMPLES

- *Yo:* Very informal word for *hey.*
- *Dude/Man/Bro:* Slang words young men call each other.
- *That sucks:* Very informal to mean something is unpleasant.
- *Imma:* Extremely informal slang that means *I'm going to.*

MORE INFORMAL YOUTHFUL SLANG

- *Finna:* going to. In the southern states, it is translated to another slang that also means going to, *fixin' to.*
- *Sus:* abbreviation for suspicious.
- *Bussin':* something is very good- usually used with food.
- *To be shook:* to be in shock.

The Play.

<Rose: I can't believe I got a part in the play!
<Aria: Congrats! How long did you practice for your audition?
<Rose: That's the thing! I actually didn't have any time to prepare, and just **winged it!**
<Aria: No way! You're a natural Rose! I'm so happy for you!
<Rose: Thank you! I can't wait for the play!
<Aria: You're gonna knock'em dead!

Rose is shocked that she got the part because she didn't prepare.

VOCABULARY & EXTRA EXAMPLES

- *Thats the thing:* used to introduce a point of discussion.
- *To be a natural at something:* to have instinctive talent for something.
- *I can't wait:* to be eager for something to begin or to happen.
- *Knock'em dead:* impress them.

CULTURE TIP

*We let others know we are winging something so that we are less likely to receive judgment from others since they will know that we haven't prepared. We hope that they are more forgiving of us if we make a mistake since we are **winging it.**

SIMILAR EXPRESSIONS

- I don't have a plan for today, lets just **play it by ear.**
- I'm so glad you like it! I just **threw it together** last minute.
- She didn't bring the dog's food, so we'll have to **improvise.**

TO BE GOOD TO GO

DEFINITION: TO BE READY.

Late.

<Nick: Jess, come on! We can't be late! Let's go!
<Jessie: I just need to fix my hair and I'll be down.
<Nick: Honey, I'm sure it already looks great. I really don't want to be late!
<Jessie: Hey, while I'm flat ironing my hair, will you make me a coffe to go?
<Nick: Ok. How many shots do you want?
<Jessie: 2 shots please, and I'd like it in my pink tumbler please.
<Nick: Ok, but please hurry!
*10 minutes later
<Jessie: See, no need to get all upset. I'm dressed, coffee is made, and presents are already in the car. We're **good to go**!

Nick and Jessie are going to a party. Nick is worried that Jessie will make them late. Surprisingly, she is on time and ready to leave for the party.

VOCABULARY & EXTRA EXAMPLES

• *Come on:* slang for *let's go.*

• *To flat iron:* to straighten one's hair.

• *Coffee to go:* coffee made to drink not at home; portable.

• *Tumbler:* an insulated bottle that keeps liquid hot or cold for hours, it also has a lid and is portable.

Benny The Mechanic.

<Rex: Hey Benny! How's the car? Did you get it all fixed up?
<Benny: Yes sir. Those squeaky brakes gave me a run for my money, but I got it sorted out. New radiator, changed the oil, and even rotated the tires. You're **good to go**!
<Rex: Thanks Benny! How much do I owe ya?
<Benny: Nothin' man. This one is on me.
<Rex: No, Benny, I insist!
<Benny: Rex, your money is no good here. Tell Jane and the kids we say hello!

Benny fixes his friend Rex's car for free.

VOCABULARY & EXTRA EXAMPLES

- *All fixed up:* everything has been adjusted or fixed.
- *Squeaky brakes:* the sound describes defective car brakes.
- *A run for my money:* to make something difficult for someone to accomplish or to be good competition.
- *To sort something out:* to resolve a difficulty or a problem.
- *Ya:* slang for *you.*
- *Your money is no good here / This one is on me:* both expressions are used when one completes a service, or will buy something for someone for free.

MORE WAYS TO SAY I'M GOOD TO GO:

- *I'm **all set**. Let's go ahead and leave for the play.*
- *I'm **ready now**, so I'll meet you there.*
- *I'm finally **done** with my project. Time to relax!*

JESSICA SMITH

TO FEAST ONE'S EYES ON

DEFINITION: TO LOOK AT SOMETHING WITH GREAT PLEASURE.

***CAUTION:** ONLY USE WITH PEOPLE IN A BRAGGING MANNER. WE DO NOT USE THIS EXPRESSION WITH CHILDREN BECAUSE IT WOULD IMPLY SOMETHING IMPURE OR SEXUAL.

All A's.

<Stella: I got my report card at school today!
<Mom: Oh yeah? How did you do??
<Stella: (*Stella pulls out her report card to show to Mom.*) **Feast your eyes on** this! I got all A's!
<Mom: That's wonderful honey! I'm so proud of you!

Stella and Mom are proud of Stella's achievements at school.

VOCABULARY & EXTRA EXAMPLES

- *All A's:* The grading system in the USA uses letters A-F. An A is the highest grade attainable.

EVEN MORE EXPRESSIONS WITH "EYES"

- *Eyes on the prize:* to stay focused on one's goals.

    Just keep your **eyes on the prize**, I know you can win this race!
- *A sight for sore eyes:* A person or thing one is happy and relieved to see.

    Aren't you **a sight for sore eyes**! I've missed you so much!

• *Keep an eye on:* To keep under careful observation.
  *You go get some dinner. I'll **keep an eye on** the kids.*

Spectacular.

\<Curtis: I'm so glad you were free to take a hike with me.
\<Violet: Me too. I've always wanted to hike this trail, but I'm just always so busy!
\<Curtis: I know what you mean.
\<Violet: Ok, almost to the top!
\<Curtis: Just wait for it, you're going to be blown away. Come over here. Look! Just **feast your eyes on** that sunset! Isn't it gorgeous??
\<Violet: Wow! It's spectacular!! Absolutely stunning!

Curtis is excited to show the magnificent sunset to Violet.

A FURTHER EXPLANATION

When we **feast our eyes on** something, it is something that is special or amazing. By using this expression, we are bragging about something or someone. Here are more adjectives to describe beautiful or awesome things or people:
• Magnificent.
• Second to none.
• Marvelous.
• Staggering.
• Phenomenal.
• Lovely.
• Breathtaking.

TO SCOOT OVER

DEFINITION: TO SLIGHTLY MOVE TO THE SIDE TO MAKE MORE ROOM.

Mom's Night.

<Sophie: Hey Ava! I'm so glad you made it.
<Ava: Yeah, me too. Traffic was crazy!
<Sophie: Come sit down. There is plenty of room. Hey Emily, could you please **scoot over** so Ava can fit?
<Emily: Sure, no problem!
<Ava: Thanks! So excited to finally get together for dinner!

Ava is late to meet her friends for dinner due to heavy traffic. Ava asks Emily to move over a bit to make more room for Sophie to sit down.

Join In.

<James: Hey man! What are you guys doing here?
<Daniel: Hey James! Just getting some lunch, you wanna join?
<James: You sure you don't mind?
<Daniel: Nah man! Here take my seat. Guys, **scoot over** so I can fit another chair at the table for James!

James sees his friend Daniel at a restaurant getting lunch. Daniel invites James to join him and his friends for lunch. After James accepts the invitation to join, Daniel asks the other friends to scoot over in order to make more room for another chair at the table for James.

Hustle Up.

<Coach Tom: Everyone on the bench. We need to talk about Saturday's game. Hustle up!
<Simon: **Scoot down** Alex! There's not enough room for me!
<Alex: Dude, calm down. There is plenty room for you!
<Coach Tom: What's the problem here men?
<Simon: Nothing.
<Alex: All's good Coach.
<Coach: Why are you still standing Simon? Sit down. Alex, **scoot on down**.

Coach Tom tells everyone to go and sit on the bench. Alex will not scoot down the bench in order to make room for Simon until Coach Tom scolds him.

* When sitting on a bench, or a continuous surface such as a bench, we can also say *scoot down* or *scoot on down*.

VOCABULARY & EXTRA EXAMPLES

- *Hustle up:* hurry up; let's go!
- *Plenty:* more than enough.

MORE WAYS TO SAY SCOOT OVER

- *Scooch*
- *Scooch over*
- *Make room for*
- *Move over (not polite)*

TO STIR THE POT

DEFINITION: TO PROVOKE; TO CAUSE UNNECESSARY TROUBLE; TO AGITATE.

Drama Queen.

<Angela: I can't wait for my birthday party on Saturday!
<Pam: I know it's going to be so fun!
<Angela: Should I invite Karen?
<Pam: Are you crazy?? She's a total drama queen!
<Angela: I guess you're right, she is a drama queen.
<Pam: Duh! She is always **stirring the pot**. Remember that time she made Samantha cry by asking her about dieting ?
<Angela: Oh yeah. Let's not invite Karen.

Angela and Pam are excited about Angela's upcoming birthday party. Pam advises Angela not to invite Karen because she always "stirs the pot" and causes dissention.

SIMILAR WAYS TO SAY "STIR THE POT"

- *The class **provoked** their teacher until he lost his temper.*
- She tried to **instigate** an argument with me this morning.
- *Wherever she goes, she always **stirs up** some kind of trouble.*
- That remark really **set** him off, I've never seen him that mad.
- The opposing team **antagonized** them with insults.

Thanksgiving.

<Dad: Mia, can you bring the salt and pepper to the table?
<Mia: Sure Dad.
<Max: Dad, is Uncle Matt coming to Thanksgiving dinner?
<Dad: Yes. Don't bring up politics, you know how he loves to **stir the pot**.
<Mia and Alex: We know Dad. We remember last Thanksgiving, when he kept talking about the election just to make Aunt Tracy upset.
<Dad: Exactly. I wish he wasn't such a *pot stirrer*!
<Max: I wish he would just get a life!
<Dad: Watch it, Max.

Mia, Max, and Dad are getting ready for Thanksgiving dinner. Dad reminds his kids to be careful with Uncle Matt because he is always instigating trouble and dissention.

*Someone who continually and purposefully causes controversial trouble is referred to as a *pot stirrer*.

VOCABULARY & EXTRA EXAMPLES

• *To bring up:* to mention.
• *Get a life:* a strong disapproving insult that insinuates a person's life is too boring, that the person cares about mundane things, or that the person is a busybody.
• *Watch it:* a disapproving warning to pay attention to what one is saying, especially if it is negative.

TO DIVVY SOMETHING UP

DEFINITION: TO DIVIDE OR SHARE BETWEEN OTHERS.

Sold Out.

<Carl: Wow, I can't believe we sold so many t-shirts!
<Matt: I know! I'm in shock right now! We completely sold out!
<Thomas: It's incredible! Our t-shirts are the real deal!
<Carl: Wait til you hear this. I also got an order from the principal at Olive High School. He is going to give one to each graduate this year!
<Matt: Mind blown!
<Thomas: Are you kidding???
<Carl: I know!! We are killin' it! Let's finish packing up, and then we can **divvy up** our cash profit from today.
<Matt and Thomas: Sounds good! Let's get it done!

Carl, Matt, and Thomas are at the market selling their t-shirts. They are surprised when they completely sell out of their merchandise. As soon as they clean and pack up, they will divide or "divvy up" their profit between themselves.

VOCABULARY

• *The real deal:* extraordinary/ better than all the rest.
• *Wait till you hear this:* an expression when one is excited to get the response from another person.
• *Mind blown:* to be surprised or perplexed.

PRACTICAL AMERICAN ENGLISH

- *Are you kidding?:* another way to say *I can't believe it!*
- *Killin' it:* doing something extremely well.
- *To pack up:* to put things away.
- *Get it done:* slang to finish something.

Leftovers.

<Amanda: Wow, that was the best pizza I've ever eaten.
<Janette: Right?? Hands down, the best!
<Heather: Yeah, it was fantastic.
<Amanda: I'm so full but I still have half of mine left.
<Janette: Same here.
<Heather: Me too. You guys wanna to **divvy up** the leftovers?
<Amanda: Oh great idea!

The women go out to eat at a pizza restaurant. They are full even though they didn't finish their food. Heather suggests sharing the leftovers amongst themselves. In this way, each woman will get to try each of the pizzas.

VOCABULARY

- *Right:* slang used to agree with a statement.
- *Hands down:* without question.
- *Same here:* me too.
- *Leftovers:* extra food that wasn't eaten.

CULTURAL TIP

Scraps are different than leftovers. Scraps are fragments of food that are left on one's plate. These remnants are different than leftovers, because leftovers are excess amounts of food that can still be eaten.

* In the USA it is common and normal to ask for a *to- go* box for

JESSICA SMITH

one's leftovers at a restaurant.

TO BE A TOUGH CALL

DEFINITION: A DIFFICULT DECISION.

The Championship.

<Eddie: So, who do you think will win the championship?
<Felix: Oh man, I don't know. I've always been a fan of Miami, but this year, their team isn't looking so good.
<Eddie: Yeah, I hear ya.
<Felix: However, they do have a great offense. So maybe they could pull it off.
<Eddie: Kansas is killing it this year though!
<Felix: They are! Crazy. I can't decide between the two. It's **a tough call**.

Friends Eddie and Felix are discussing who will win the national championship. Eddie suggests that the winner may be Kansas, but Felix is still unsure. He can't decide who he thinks will win.

VOCABULARY
- *Isn't looking good:* seemingly defected or ill.
- *To pull it off:* to succeed at something.
- *Killing it:* doing something very well.

Shopping.

<Tracy: I'm so excited for the party this weekend!
<Diana: I know me too! It's gonna be a blast.
<Tracy: Ok, so which dress are you gonna buy?
<Diana: Oh, I can't decide! I love the way this blue one fits.
<Tracy: Yeah, it fits like a glove!
<Diana: Exactly! However, it's kinda overpriced. I really like this yellow one too, but I don't love it- you know what I mean?
<Tracy: Yeah, totally. That's **a tough call!**

Friends Tracy and Diana are shopping for Diana's new dress for the party this weekend. Diana is trying to decide between two dresses.

VOCABULARY

- *Fits like a glove:* to be the right size, or to be well suited for something.
- *Overpriced:* costing more than it's worth.
- *You know what I mean:* suggests that the person listening completely understands and doesn't need more of an explanation.

DECISION VOCABULARY

- *That's a hard pass:* No way!
- *Let me think about it:* It's a possibility.
- *I need to weigh the pros and cons:* needing to consider the advantages and disadvantages of both possible decisions.
- *I need to sleep on it:* I'm not sure, and need the rest of the day and night to make my decision.
- *Make up your mind!:* Decide!

◆ ◆ ◆

TO BE FLOORED

DEFINITION: TO BE SHOCKED.

Olivia And Tom.

<Jane: Did you hear about Olivia and Tom?
<Rachel: No! What? Did something happen? Are they ok?
<Jane: Well, I wouldn't say that they are ok.
<Rachel: What?? Spit it out!
<Jane: Olivia left him. She found out that he's been cheating on her for months with his secretary.
<Rachel: No way. Are you serious? She's like 21 years old!
<Jane: I'm dead serious. It's so twisted.
<Rachel: Wow. I don't even know what to say.
<Jane: I was absolutely **floored** when she told me. I still can't believe it!

Jane tells Rachel that their friend Olivia left her husband since finding out that he has been unfaithful to her for several months. Both Jane and Rachel are shocked, and in disbelief.

VOCABULARY

- *To spit it out:* an urge to confess or reveal something.
- *To cheat on:* to be unfaithful in a relationship.
- *Dead serious:* absolutely serious.
- *Twisted:* abnormal, warped, perverted, evil.

New Adventures.

<Mr. Smith: Honey, I have something to tell you.
<Mrs. Smith: Ok...
<Mr. Smith: Today, I sold most of our stocks, and I took a leave of absence from work.
<Mrs. Smith: Wait, what? Are you for real?
<Mr. Smith: Yes. 100 percent. I need adventure in our lives again, Wendy. I say we sell this big old house, take our money, and travel, just like we've always wanted to do! What do you think?
<Mrs. Smith: I don't know what to think, Kevin. I'm **floored**. I can't believe you took a leave of absence from work!
<Mr. Smith: I know it's extreme, but we've wanted to do this for some time now. The kids are grown, you are retired, what are we waiting on???

Mr. and Mrs. Smith have been married for many years. One day, Mr. Smith reveals that he has taken a leave of absence from work, because he wants to take a break from their normal life, to travel and make memories together. Mrs. Smith is shocked.

VOCABULARY

• *Stocks:* a share of a company.

• *To take a leave of absence from one's job:* a way to take unpaid time off of work due to unusual circumstances.

• *Are you for real?:* Are you serious?

• *To be retired:* to permanently leave the work force usually due to old age.

TO GROW ON SOMEONE

DEFINITION: TO BEGIN TO LIKE SOMETHING.

New Hair.

<Kelly: Hey Emma! I've missed you so much!
<Emma: Hey friend! I've missed you too!
<Kelly: I wanna hear everything! You've gotta tell me more about your job, and your uptight boss. Oh, and I gotta know what ended up happening with your Italian neighbor's cat!
<Emma: We have so much to catch up on!
<Kelly: We totally do! By the way, do you like my new haircut?
<Emma: Of course I do! You know I loved your long hair, but the sling is growing on me!

Kelly and Emma discuss Kelly's new haircut.

VOCABULARY

- *Hey friend:* an endearing way to greet a friend.
- *Wanna:* want to.
- *Gotta:* got to.
- *To be uptight:* to be tense, controlling, angry, and anxious.
- *Ended up:* to eventually be in a particular situation, place, or state after a series of happenings.
- *To catch up on:* to learn and discuss what has been happening.

- *A sling haircut:* a haircut that is shorter in the back than the front. It's also referred to as a *bob*.

❖ ❖ ❖

City Life.

<Rocky: How's the big city treating you?
<Bruno: It's alright. I can't complain.
<Rocky: How do you sleep at night with all of that city racket?
<Bruno: Yeah, its definitely loud.
<Rocky: You ever think about moving back home?
<Bruno: You know, I used to, but now, the city is **growing on me**. The crowds of people are still a shock to me, but overall I'm really starting to like it here.
<Rocky: Thats great man. I'm happy for you!

Rocky and Bruno are talking on the phone. The men grew up together, and Bruno has moved away to the big city. Rocky asks if he will move back home to the country. Bruno confesses that he is really starting to like the city.

VOCABULARY

- *How's it treating you:* a way to ask if one likes something, or someone in one's life.
- *I can't complain:* nothing serious is wrong; everything is ok.
- *Racket:* loud unpleasant noise.

EXTRA EXAMPLES

- My new glasses are **growing on** me.
- Try the tea again, it has to **grow on** you.
- At first, I didn't like the her personality, but it **grew on** me.
- She isn't fond of bold colors, but this blue room is **growing on** her.

TO MILK IT

DEFINITION: TO TAKE ADVANTAGE OF A SITUATION.

Rest While You Can.

<Rose: Hey Stacy. I'm calling to let you know that I won't be able to make it tonight.
<Stacy: Oh no! You ok?
<Rose: I'm ok. I was just up all night with a fever.
<Stacy: Oh girl, I am so sorry! I hope you feel better soon! Was Andy able to take off to watch the kids?
<Rose: Yes, thankfully! I can hear them all downstairs playing.
<Stacy: Ok good! I hope you feel better soon! Hey maybe you should **milk it** for a couple extra days of rest!
<Rose: Haha I was already thinking the same thing! It's nice to rest and to be waited on, even if I am sick!
<Stacy: Exactly! Alright Rose, you take care! Let me know if you need anything!
<Rose: Thanks Stacy!

Rose and Stacy had plans for this evening. Unfortunately, Rose becomes sick. She calls Stacy to cancel her plans. Stacy advises Rose to take advantage of the situation, so that she can rest even longer than she actually needs to.

VOCABULARY

- *Let you know:* to update someone on circumstances.
- *To take off work:* to stay home from work.
- *To be waited on:* to be served and taken care of.

Disgusting.

<Zoe: Did you read that article about our favorite actress, Lea?
<Noel: Oh yeah, I feel so sorry for her!
<Zoe: Me too! Poor woman doesn't have any privacy.
<Noel: Zilch! The media is really **milking the story** for all it's worth.
<Zoe: Oh, I know! I've seen it on every site and channel.
<Noel: It's all about money for them. Disgusting.
<Zoe: I couldn't agree more!

Zoe and Noel discuss an article that exposes something negative about their favorite actress. The two women agree that the story is taking advantage of the woman's fame for profit.

VOCABULARY

- *To feel sorry for someone:* to pity someone.
- *Zilch:* none.
- *For all it's worth:* as much as possible.

SIMILAR EXPRESSIONS TO MILK IT

- *To suck/or to bleed someone or something dry:* to take or command every good resource until there isn't any left.

    *The company **sucks** their employees **dry** for a couple of years, and then fires them.*

- *To exploit:* to use selfishly for one's own benefit.

    *She **exploited** the town's lack of resources to grow her business.*

- *To cash in on*: to use an opportunity for profit.

    *Relators are **cashing in on** the influx of buyers from California.*

JESSICA SMITH

TO TAKE A CRACK AT IT

DEFINITION: TO TRY DO SOMETHING.

Pops And Son.

<Gene: I just can't seem to get this new microwave installed.
<Owen: Here Pops, let me **take a crack at it**. There! I got it!
<Gene: Terrific my boy! Thank you, son!
<Owen: Happy to help, sir.

Gene and his son Owen are installing a new microwave. Gene is having trouble, so Owen tries and succeeds.

UNDERSTANDING TITLES IN THE USA

- Sir : This is a respectful way to address a man. We also use this term to address a man that we don't know. For example: *Excuse me sir, where can I find the paint brushes?*

- Mr. : This is another respectful way to address a man. However the difference is that it is a man that we know, since the last name is used in combination with *Mr.* For example: *Mr. Smith*, or *Mr. Jones*.

- Mrs. : This title is for married women of any age. It is used in combination with her last name. *Mrs. Smith*, or *Mrs. Jones*.

- Ms. : Most commonly, this title is used for women who have been divorced or widowed. It also can be used to address women whose marital status is unknown. it is used in combination with the woman's last name: *Ms. Hall*, or *Ms. Kinney*.

- Miss : This title is most commonly used in combination with a young unmarried woman's last name, or by itself. *You dropped your scarf miss. Miss Fox will help you with the paperwork.* It also can be used in combination with a woman's first name as a term of respect with children. This is most common in the southern states in the USA. For example, *Miss Kate will help you clean up.*
- Ma'am : This term is used when we do not know a woman. It is not combined with her last or first name. It's also used as a term of respect for all women. There is no exact age, but it is usually used with women 40 years and older.

It's A Date!

\<Danny: You wanna meet me for a round of golf this Saturday?
\<Brittney: You know I've never played golf before, right?
\<Danny: Never? Really? I was sure that you had!
\<Brittney: No, but I'm a quick learner, so I'll **take a crack at it**.
\<Danny: Alright! Sounds great. Meet me there at 10am?
\<Brittney: See you then!

Danny invites Brittney to play golf with him on Saturday. They decide to meet at 10am.

ADDITIONAL EXAMPLES

- *I have no idea how to change a tire, but I'll **take a crack at it**!*
- *Let me **take a crack at it**!*
- *He **took a crack at it**, but couldn't figure it out.*
- *They **took a crack at it**, but couldn't figure out the code.*
- *Can you lend her your fishing pole, so she can **take a crack at it**?*

TO RUFFLE SOMEONE'S FEATHERS.

DEFINITION: TO CAUSE SOMEONE TO BE UPSET OR ANNOYED.

Rude.

<Parker: Hey Tiffany, are you ok?
<Tiffany: Yeah, I'm fine, how come? Oh, you mean because of what Jackson said during the meeting?
<Parker: Yeah girl, you sure you're ok? He's the worst!
<Tiffany: Yeah, I'm ok now. I shouldn't have gotten so upset, especially since I know he was doing it on purpose just **to ruffle my feathers**. He's such a jerk.
<Parker: I agree. My jaw dropped when he said it. I'm so sorry!
<Tiffany: Thanks Parker, I really appreciate that. Wanna grab a coffee and check out that new book store?
<Parker: I would love that!

Parker checks to see if her friend Tiffany is ok after their coworker Jackson was rude to her in the meeting. Tiffany knows that Jackson was purposefully trying to upset her.

VOCABULARY

- *How come:* another way to ask *why.*
- *Jerk:* a term to describe a rude, cruel, or small minded person.

- *My jaw dropped:* an expression used when one is shocked.
- *Grab a coffee: grab* is often used to mean *to get.*

* If we say someone or something is "the worst," it means that we dislike or even hate something or someone very much. In the same respect, if we say something is "the best," we are praising how good something or someone is.

Oh Snap.

\<Eva: Hey Liam! Did you hear about the mayor's speech?
\<Liam: Oh yeah, everyone is talking about it!
\<Eva: I guess he **ruffled** quite a few **feathers** going on and on about climate change.
\<Liam: What was he thinking?!
\<Eva: Well, I heard that it was all for show. He is supposed to get a kick back from some big company for this meeting promoting climate change.
\<Liam: Oh snap! Seriously?
\<Eva: That's the word on the street right now.
\<Liam: Sheesh. I guess I wouldn't put it past him.
\<Eva: My thoughts exactly.

Eva tells Liam about the mayor upsetting everyone at the town meeting. She also shares the gossip concerning the mayor's true motives.

VOCABULARY

- *To go on and on:* to continue for a long time without stopping; usually something that's boring or unpleasant.
- *All for show:* merely for appearance; not genuine or sincere.
- *A kick back:* money paid in exchange for a service.

- *Oh snap:* slang exclamation for shock or surprise
- *The word on the street:* the rumor.
- *Sheesh:* expresses disappointment, surprise, or annoyance.
- *Wouldn't put it past someone:* someone is capable of wrongdoing.
- *My thoughts exactly:* another way to say, *I agree.*

TO TABLE IT

DEFINITION: TO POSTPONE UNTIL LATER.

Figured Out.

<Esme: Look I really can't talk about this anymore. I'm exhausted. Can't we just **table it** until later?
<Verity: I wish, but remember the meeting is tomorrow. Jane said the boss will be here at 8 sharp. We have to get this sorted out so I can advise the others before the end of the day.
<Esme: You're right. Let's keep trying to figure something out.
<Verity: We'll come up with something. We've got this.

Esme and Verity are trying to make some important decisions that include their colleagues because the boss comes for the meeting tomorrow.

VOCABULARY

- *8 sharp:* exactly at 8:00.
- *To sort something out:* to resolve a problem or difficulty.
- *To figure something out:* to find a solution or make a decision.
  - *I'm trying **to figure out** what to wear to the concert.*
  - *He **figured out** that his dog only eats on the rug.*
  - *We are trying **to figure out** where to park.*

MORE WAYS TO SAY LET'S WAIT

- *I'm **putting off** studying until Thursday. I don't want to do it right now.*
- *They had to **postpone** the wedding due to the storm.*

• We should **hold off on** buying a new car until we have the cash.

The Party.

<Liam: I disagree. Mel and Niles won't be able to make it, so we should postpone the party until next weekend.
<Katie: I know you want them to come, but it will be a pain to postpone. Also, the weather is supposed to be beautiful, and I'm off work that Friday!
<Liam: We've been discussing this for an hour. Can't we just **table it** for now, and make a decision later? I have a headache.
<Katie: Fine.

Liam and Katie are in a disagreement over the date of their party. They decide to make an agreement later.

IDIOMS ABOUT WAITING
- *Hurry up and wait:* to move quickly, and then be forced to wait.
- *Don't hold your breath:* don't expect something to happen for a long time.
- *Stick around:* to wait somewhere.
- *To kill time:* to wait and waste time.

HOW TO ASK SOMEONE TO WAIT
- *Please bear with me.*
- *Just a moment please.*
- *Excuse me for a moment.*
- *Hold on a minute/second.*
- *Hang on a minute/second.* (Informal.)
- *Hold up.* (Informal slang.)
- *Give me a minute/second.* (Very informal).
- *Hold your horses!* (Very informal.)

JESSICA SMITH

TO BE A DUD

DEFINITION: SOMETHING IS DEFECTIVE OR UNSATISFACTORY.
SYNONYM: A LEMON.

That's Bizarre.

<Caroline: Hey, wanna see the new watch I ordered Eddie?
<Jimmy: Oh yeah, I want to see it! I need to find him a gift too, but he's such an oddball. I can't decide what to get him.
<Caroline: What in the world?? That's bizarre. I know I plugged my phone up to charge before coming over here. Why is it almost dead?
<Jimmy: Maybe you didn't have it plugged in good?
<Caroline: No, look it's plugged up right now, and its not charging. This is my new charger! I just got it on Monday!
<Jimmy: Ugh. I'm sorry Caroline. Looks like its a **dud**.
<Caroline: It figures.
<Jimmy: Come on, let's go to the store, I'll drive.

Caroline tells Jimmy that she finally got her new charger, but that it suddenly stopped working shortly after purchasing it.

VOCABULARY

- *Wanna:* slang for *want to.*
- *To be an oddball:* to be eccentric, unusual, or strange.
- *What in the world:* a polite way to express shock.
- *Bizarre:* Odd, strange.
- *To come over:* to go from one place to another.

- *Looks like:* a way to say, *It seems as if.*
- *It figures:* idiom to mean that one isn't surprised.

It's A Lemon.

\<Elle: I think our dishwasher is a **lemon**.
\<Phillip: Right?!
\<Elle: This is the second time that I've opened it and found dirty dishes, when they were supposed to be clean.
\<Phillip: Such a pain in the neck! I came home from work yesterday and there was a huge puddle under it.
\<Elle: No way! So have you already tried to fix it?
\<Phillip: Yes, I've tried, but I'm thinking we're fighting a losing battle with this thing.

Elle and Phillip realize that their dishwasher is defected.

IDIOMS ABOUT DIFFICULTY

- *At my wit's end:* frustrated and unable to solve a problem
*I'm **at my wit's end** with the new babysitter. She has been late everyday this week!*

- *To dodge a bullet*: to avoid a serious problem or situation.
*She really **dodged a bullet** not marrying Tim!*

- *Grasping at straws:* to be desperate.
*He was **grasping** at straws trying to explain why he was stealing.*

- *An uphill battle*: to struggle against many unfavorable circumstances in order to achieve a goal.
*The new boss is fighting **an uphill battle** to restore the reputation of*

the company.

TO THROW IN THE TOWEL

DEFINITION: TO QUIT IN DEFEAT.
SYNONYM: TO GIVE UP.

Overwhelmed.

<Luke: I don't think we're gonna finish this project on time.
<Peter: Yeah, this is rough. I didn't hear back from Tony until yesterday, and Mac wants everything wrapped up by Thursday. I just don't see how we're gonna get it done.
<Luke: Yeah, I'm overwhelmed. Tony really threw a wrench in it, because we were so close to being finished. I didn't realize he would send so much data!
<Peter: It also doesn't help that Violet and Matt are on vacay.
<Luke: Well, we can't just **throw in the towel**. You wanna go grab a bite to eat, and hit it hard when we come back?
<Peter: Yeah, let's do it. I need a break.

Luke and Peter are at work trying to finish a project on time.

VOCABULARY

- *Rough:* used to describe a difficult situation.
- *To hear back from someone:* to receive a response from someone.
- *To wrap something up:* to finish something.
- *I can't see how:* I don't know or understand how.
- *To be overwhelmed:* to have a strong emotional effect- can be

positive or negative.

- *To throw a wrench in something:* to make something more difficult, or to ruin it.
- *Vacay:* short for vacation.
- *Hit it hard:* to work hard to accomplish something.
- *A break*: to stop doing something for a short time.

Fresh Eyes.

\<Iris: I'm done with my painting.
\<Hugo: Oh yeah? You finished it?
\<Iris: Nope. I can't figure it out, and I refuse to spend even one more minute on it. I'm **throwing in the towel**.
\<Hugo: No, Iris! Don't quit. You've put so much time and energy into it. Just take a break and come back to it with fresh eyes in the morning.
\<Iris: Maybe you're right. I'm not a quitter.
\<Hugo: No you're not. That's what I love about you.

Iris is so frustrated with her painting, but Hugo encourages her to not give up.

EXPRESSIONS

- *To figure something out:* to solve a problem.
- *Fresh eyes:* refers to eyes that aren't biased.

MORE EXPRESSIONS THAT MEAN DON'T GIVE UP

- **Hang in there**, it'll get bettter soon!
- Learning a new sport is hard, but just **stick with it!**
- I'm sure if you **give it some time**, they will be more relaxed.

JESSICA SMITH

TO SHOOT THE BREEZE

DEFINITION: VERY CASUAL FRIENDLY CONVERSATION.
*SYNONYMS: CHITCHAT; CHAT; GAB.

Old Times.

<Otto: I really enjoyed just **shootin' the breeze** with ya tonight.
<Theo: Yeah it was like old times.
<Otto: It was. We need to do it more often.
<Theo: Ya'll wanna come over next week for supper?
<Otto: We'd love to. We're free Sunday evening. We can bring over some fresh corn from the garden, and Hayley's famous blackberry cobbler. How's that sound?
<Theo: My mouth is waterin' already! I'm looking forward to it.
<Otto: Us too!

Old friends Otto and Theo shoot the breeze all evening.

VOCABULARY

- *Ya:* slang for *you.*
- *Old times:* used when reminiscing good memories in the past.
- *Ya'll:* slang used in the south of the USA, to mean *you all.*
- *Supper:* slang used in the south of the USA to mean *"dinner."*
- *Famous:* slang to mean very well liked; not actually famous.
- *How's that sound:* slang for, *"What do you think?"*

• *My mouth is waterin':* an expression to describe the feeling of being excited to eat something.

Grannie And Gramps.

<Clara: I'm really happy we came to visit.
<Luna: Me too. I've really missed Grannie and Gramps.
<Clara: They really are so special.
<Luna: Grannie and I just sat on the front porch **shootin' the breeze** until almost 9:00!
<Clara: She's the best! I was wondering what you guys were doing while Gramps and I were weeding out the garden.
<Luna: We just talked about anything and everything. She's so wise, but also, still such a firecracker!
<Clara: I know right? Gramps had me cracking up while we were working in the garden.
<Luna: He's a silly old goofball. I love them both so much!

Luna and Clara are enjoying their visit with their grandparents.

VOCABULARY

• *Grannie and Gramps:* Grandmother and Grandfather.

• *To weed out:* to remove the weeds.

• *Anything and everything:* a way to say nothing is off limits.

• *A firecracker:* used to describe high spirited, bold, confident people who aren't afraid to say what they think.

• *I know right:* popular slang that means one strongly agrees.

SYNONYMS FOR SHOOTIN' THE BREEZE

• They always **chitchat** a bit when they see each other at work.

• We had a nice **chat** while drinking our coffee on the balcony.

- He likes to **gab** more than his sister.

TO CALL IT A DAY

DEFINITION: TO STOP AN ACTIVITY FOR THE REST OF THE DAY.

It's 5 O'clock.

<Finn: Wow, I can't believe it's already 5 o'clock.
<Eleanor: No way! It's 5 o'clock?!
<Finn: Yep. It's time **to call it a day.**
<Eleanor: Finally! I gotta shut everything down. I also need to check with Angela about the office party tomorrow. It completely slipped my mind to tell her we're bringing cookies instead of chips.
<Finn: Alright, I'll be out in the car. Do you wanna stop at the store on the way home? I'm outta coffee beans.
<Eleanor: Yeah, sounds good! I need to grab some milk while we're there too. Don't let me forget!

Husband and wife, Eleanor and Finn, who work together in the same office finish working for the day.

VOCABULARY

- *Yep:* Yes.
- *Gotta:* have to or must.
- *To shut everything down:* to turn off electronics.
- *To slip one's mind:* to forget.
- *Outta:* out of.
- *To be outta something:* to not have any more of something.
- *To grab:* slang *to get* or *to acquire.*

Brain Fried.

<Oscar: Hey did you get that nasty email from Sam?
<Jude: Yeah, what's gotten him all riled up?
<Oscar: I guess he's still peeved about getting passed over for that promotion?
<Jude: He needs to let that go, and move on already.
<Oscar: Yeah, but he won't. You know how uptight he is.
<Jude: This project is a mess! I'm shocked that they even accepted Tim's pitch last week.
<Oscar: I know! I think I'm done for today. I have a headache.
<Jude: Yeah dude, let's **call it a day**. My brain is fried.
<Oscar: Same. Let's go.

Colleagues Oscar and Jude are working on a project, and having trouble with it. They decide to quit working for the evening.

VOCABULARY

- *Nasty:* mean or ill willed.
- *All riled up:* agitated.
- *Peeved:* very angry or annoyed.
- *To move on:* to accept that something has changed, and to begin something new.
- *Uptight:* someone who is tense, nervous, or uneasy.
- *To be a mess:* to be unorganized.
- *A pitch:* another term for a business proposal.
- *Dude:* slang term for a male friend.
- *One's brain is fried:* to be mentally exhausted.
- *Same:* slang for "mine/me too."

JESSICA SMITH

❖ ❖ ❖

TO NAIL IT

DEFINITION: TO ACHIEVE OR TO SUCCEED AT SOMETHING.

*THIS EXPRESSION IS ALSO USED SARCASTICALLY AND COMICALLY TO MEAN THE OPPOSITE DEFINITION- TO FAIL.

Time To Celebrate.

<Sienna: How did you do on the test??
<Adel: I **nailed it**!
<Sienna: Awesome, me too!
<Adel: Let's go shopping to celebrate!
<Sienna: I'm down!! I've been wanting to go for so long. Let's try that new sushi place for dinner afterwards.
<Adel: Oh great idea! Before we get going, will you pop the trunk, I need to check in my backpack. I want to be sure that I grabbed my science book.
<Sienna: Sure thing. Actually while we're at it, I want to check under the hood too.
<Adel: Ok, I got my book, everything ok under the hood?
<Sienna: Yep, all good! Buckle up, let's go!

Two friends Adel and Sienna are happy to have done well on their exam, and go out to celebrate their success.

VOCABULARY

• *I'm down:* a way to agree and commit to something. One can also say *"I'm in,"* or *"I'm up for it."*
• *Pop the trunk:* open the hatch.

- *To check under the hood:* to check the vehicle's engine, or other parts under the hood of the vehicle.
- *Sure thing:* a way to say *"yes, of course."*
- *While we're at it:* at the same time.

Craft Time.

\<Piper: Look at how good my wreath turned out!
\<Hazel: Wow! It's beautiful!
\<Piper: Let me see yours! Oh......what happened? Did you have some trouble?
\<Hazel: Yeah, I had a lot of trouble! It's falling apart! Also, I think I chose the wrong kind of flowers, because they aren't very sturdy. It doesn't even look like a wreath. **Nailed it**!
\<Piper: Oh Hazel! Here, let me give you a hand.
\<Hazel: Thanks girl! I guess I'm just not very good at making wreaths, or crafts in general for that matter.

Friends Piper and Hazel are making wreaths. Piper's wreath is beautiful, but Hazel's wreath looks terrible. She laughs at her failure by sarcastically saying, "Nailed it."

VOCABULARY
- *To turn out:* the way that something or someone is proven to be; the result.
- *Sturdy:* strong.
- *To give someone a hand:* to help someone.
- *Craft:* something made by hand in a skilled way.

ANTONYMS OF NAILED IT
- They **bombed** that test.
- She **failed** to create an interesting logo.

- Sales **fell short** of our expectations.
- He **struck out** at another job interview.
- I was **unsuccessful** in providing the necessary information.

TO KEEP SOMEONE POSTED

DEFINITION: TO INFORM SOMEONE OF CHANGES OR UPDATES.

Moving.

<Dax: What are you up to this weekend?
<Andy: Well, the kids have soccer practice. Why, what's up?
<Dax: A new family at my church needs help moving on Saturday. I wanted to see if you could come and help us out.
<Andy: Gotcha. Do you know what time?
<Dax: They said the moving truck would be there at 8am .
<Andy: Ok, let me talk it over with Amanda, and I'll let you know. I also have a couple of big projects this week to finish, and I'm going out of town Wednesday for a conference. I'd love to help, but it's a busy week.
<Dax: Totally understand. Just **keep me posted.** No worries if you can't! I'm gonna ask some other guys too.

Dax asks Andy to come and help a family move. Andy responds that he will see how the week goes, and then update him on whether or not he can help.

VOCABULARY

• *What are you up to:* another way to ask, "What are you doing?," or "Do you have any plans?"
• *What's up:* can be used as a greeting or as a way to ask "Is

something wrong?" or *"What do you need?"*
- *Was gonna:* was going to.
- *Gotcha:* I understand.
- *Pretty sure:* indicates a bit of doubt.
- *Let you know:* I'll confirm at a later time.

◆ ◆ ◆

You Bring The Steaks.

\<Jonathan: Hey man. How's it goin'?
\<David: All is well.
\<Jonathan: How's that back porch coming along? You gonna have me over to see it any time soon?
\<David: I've almost got it finished. I still need to stain it, but you definitely need to come and see it. We can grill out and shoot the breeze.
\<Jonathan: That's what I'm talkin' about.
\<David: I'll **keep you posted**! You can bring the steaks.
\<Jonathan: I hear ya!

David and Jonathan are discussing David's new porch that he is building. David says he will inform Jonathan when it's done so they can enjoy it together by grilling out.

VOCABULARY

- *How's it going:* an informal greeting.
- *Coming along:* asks the completion status of something.
- *That's what I'm talking about:* used to strongly agree about something.

MORE WAYS TO SAY " I'LL KEEP YOU POSTED."
- *I'll* **touch base** *with you once I have the hotel booked.*

- *Thanks for **keeping me in the loop** regarding the plans!*
- *She **kept them updated** on her progress.*
- *We haven't decided yet. We'll **let you know** by tomorrow.*

STORIES

MR. GREEN & MS. RUDDY.

Mr. Green lives on Mulberry street in a big blue house with a garden full of daisies, tulips, and quite a few turnips. His favorite hobby is relaxing in his hammock with his doxie Dante. Dante is a **chipper** little guy. He is always curious, and sometimes downright **nosey**. He keeps Mr. Green *on his toes*.

Mr. Green started his morning as usual around 11:00 am., with a cup of English tea, 2 lumps of sugar, and his newspaper. He was only on page two when Dante poked his head out from under the covers, and *waddled over* towards the back door. This could only mean one thing, Ms. Ruddy was on her way over.

Mr. Green was quite the **night owl**, and was just *getting his bearings*, whereas, Ms. Ruddy was quite the **early bird** and was *already winding down* for the day. Dante *paced back and forth* by the back screen door, watching Ms. Ruddy as she opened Mr. Tacott's back gate, and made her way to greet him. Mr. Green welcomed Ms. Ruddy into the kitchen.

<Mr. Green: Aren't you **bright eyed and bushy tailed** this morning!
<Ms. Ruddy: Morning? It's almost noon Mr. Green!
<Mr. Green: *To each his own* Ms. Ruddy.
<Ms. Ruddy: Very well. I wanted to ask if you've met our new neighbor, Darcy, yet. She's the one two doors down from Tom across the street. She lives in Franny's old house. Remember? She's very beautiful, actually, an absolute **knockout**.
<Mr. Green: Yes, Ms. Ruddy, I remember.

<Ms. Ruddy: Well, I just learned that before moving here, she actually inherited her uncle's beet farm over near Jordan Lake. You know the one I'm speaking of right?
<Mr. Green: *Well, I'll be.*
<Ms. Ruddy: Tom told me she invited him over for lunch last Wednesday, and that he couldn't get out of there fast enough. He said she was such a **negative Nancy**. Even with all of that wealth. Can you imagine? Tom said she complained the entire lunch about her move, and her new job.
<Mr. Green: Reminds me of old Matilda Baker. She never did have a good thing to say. She was always worried about something. I always did my best to cheer her up. She was such **a Debbie downer**.
<Ms. Ruddy: Oh yes, I remember Matilda. Anyways, you know Tom is such a **people pleaser**, so he said that he stayed and listened politely to all of her complaints for two entire hours! He is such a nice man. I myself don't do well with such negativity.
<Mr. Green: Yes, I know Ms. Ruddy. Would you like to go for a walk with Dante and me? It's such a beautiful day. Have you seen my tulips since they bloomed?
<Ms. Ruddy: I'd love to take a walk, and I'd love to see your tulips. Let me grab my purse, I left it on the *banister*.
<Mr. Green: Don't forget your glasses on the *mantle*.

Dante *mosied on* out the back door, ready for his midday walk.

Let's Review

Ways To Describe People

- *Chipper:* cheerful and lively.
- *Nosey:* a person who pries.
- *Early bird:* someone who wakes up and is productive in the mornings.
- *Night owl:* someone who is habitually awake and active at night.
- *Bright eyed and bushy tailed:* alert, lively, and cheerful.
- *A knockout:* Very physically attractive.
- *A negative Nancy:* Someone who is always pessimistic.
- *A Debbie downer:* someone who is pessimistic and depressive.
- *A people pleaser:* someone who always tries to make everyone happy.

Additional Expressions & Verbs

- *To keep someone on their toes:* to cause someone to be alert.
- *To each his own:* one is free to choose one's likes and dislikes.
- *Well, I'll be:* an expression of surprise or astonishment.
- *Getting one's bearings:* to understand one's position.
- *Winding down:* to relax at the end of the day.
- *To waddle:* to walk with short steps and a swaying motion.
- *To pace back and forth:* To walk forward and backwards, usually in a state of stress or anxiety.
- *To mosey :* to walk in a slow leisurely manner.

Additional Vocabulary

- *Banister:* The structure of the railing and the side of the staircase.
- *Mantle:* The shelf above a fireplace.

SLEEP.

Husband and wife, Carson and Anna, had just put the kids down for bed, and were curled up together ready to watch a movie. Carson was especially **zonked** this evening. After weeks of *putting in overtime* to get everything *squared away*, everything was finally finished. He had given his presentation earlier that morning, and was absolutely elated that it was finally over. He was more than ready **to chill.**

Anna wasn't as **zapped** as her husband. Earlier that week, their SUV had finally *bitten the dust*. Now the family needed a new vehicle asap. Anna decided it was finally time to invest in a minivan. She had **stayed up** all night researching different minivan companies and models. In fact, she **pulled an all-nighter**, and eventually **dozed off** around 5:00 am. Needless to say, today, she **overslept**, and was late getting the kids to school. As soon as she got home, she *plopped down* on the couch, and took a **catnap** with the family's dog, Carl. As soon as her head hit the pillow, she was **out like a light**.

Carson and Anna talked about their busy day, and discussed the possibility of the minivan. Carson was too **exhausted** to make any more big decisions for the day, and suggested that they **sleep on it** before committing to anything. Anna agreed. She didn't blame him for being so **worn out**. Anna turned on the movie, and was enjoying her snack. All of the sudden, she heard **snoring**. She *glanced over* at Carson, and saw that he had already **fallen fast asleep**. Anna smiled. She was happy he was finally getting some **shuteye**. She switched off the TV, and *went ahead* and watched the movie on her tablet instead, using her headphones while Carson

sawed logs. Tomorrow would be Saturday, and Anna was so happy to have finally made it to the weekend.

The sun *peeked* through the blinds, *streaming in* warm, golden light. Carson rubbed his eyes, and could hear the neighbor's lawn mower across the street. He rolled over, and glanced at the clock. He couldn't believe it! It was 9:00 a.m. and his house was quiet. It seemed as if everyone was still asleep! It was such *a treat* to **sleep in** and finally **get** some rest, even if Anna did **hog the covers** last night. He chuckled realizing that he must've **slept like a log** because he couldn't even remember any of the movie from last night. In fact, it seemed as if he hadn't even moved! Anna usually complains about his **tossing and turning** during the night, but not last night! He **slept like a baby**!

Carson turned once more to check if Anna was still sleeping. Anna was *all sprawled out.* In fact her fingers were now inches away from his face as he *gripped the side* of the bed. Carson carefully pulled back the covers, and quietly tiptoed to the kitchen to make a coffee. He hoped he would be able to enjoy it before everyone else **woke up.** He *made his way to* the front door, and out onto the driveway to pick up the newspaper. He was *thumbing through it* while *sipping on* his coffee when all of the sudden, he felt a soft *tug* on his shirt. He *whipped around* in surprise to see his youngest, Isabella *smiling from ear to ear.* "Good morning sunshine," said Carson with a smile.

Let's Review

Sleep Vocabulary & Expressions

- *Zonked/Zapped/Exhausted/To be worn out:* Extremely tired.
- *To chill:* to relax.
- *To stay up:* to stay awake.
- *To pull an all-nighter:* to stay awake all night.
- *To doze off:* to drift off to sleep.
- *To oversleep:* to sleep later than intended.
- *To take a catnap:* to take a short nap during the day.
- *To be out like a light:* to fall asleep immediately.
- *To sleep on it:* to take a full night to make a decision.
- *To fall fast asleep:* to succumb to sleep; to begin to sleep.
- *To get some shuteye:* to sleep.
- *To saw logs:* to snore.
- *To sleep in:* to purposefully sleep later than usual.
- *To hog the covers:* to selfishly keep all of the bed covers.
- *To sleep like a log/ To sleep like a baby:* to sleep well.
- *To toss and turn:* to move around a lot while sleeping.

Additional Expressions & Verbs

- *Squared away:* to have everything in order.
- *A treat:* something out of the ordinary that is special and good.
- *To glance over:* to take a brief or hurried look.
- *To put in overtime:* to work more than one's usual work hours.
- *To bite the dust:* to die or to cease to function properly.
- *To plop down:* to sit down in a heavy careless way.
- *To go ahead:* to act without waiting.
- *To make it to:* to arrive at a destination- a time or place.

- *To peek:* to look in a quick or sneaky way.
- *To stream in:* to fill in a continuous current.
- *To make your way:* to move towards something until arriving.
- *To thumb through:* to turn pages quickly, searching for something.
- *To sip on something:* to take very small drinks.
- *To tug:* to slightly pull on something or someone.

OUT FOR THE EVENING.

Finally, I made it to the weekend. I was particularly excited to stay in that evening since work that week had been absolutely *grueling*. I *flung off* my bra and **got out of my work attire**, and immediately **changed into** some **comfy** clothes. I **pulled on** my favorite pair of **baggy** sweatpants, and my oversized London t-shirt. I **slipped on** my red **house shoes**, *threw my hair into* a *messy bun, grabbed* my phone, and *fell down exhausted onto* the couch. It was only 5:00 p.m. and I was ready for bed. My dappled doxie, Minnie, waddled into the room, and impatiently stretched out for me to pick her up. Minnie loves to *veg out*. Marie, my red doxie, came bounding in behind her, leaping up onto the couch, and settled in next to me.

The house was a *disaster* since I had been working so much that week, but I just couldn't *deal with it* at the moment. So, I *wrapped up* in my favorite cream plush blanket, and enjoyed the silence for a bit. I was *as snug as a bug*. I had just started *to drift off to sleep* when my phone began to buzz. It was my best friend, Monica. She was supposed to go to a work event that evening with her boyfriend Frank. Apparently, Frank suddenly *came down with* some type of stomach virus, and couldn't go. Monica really didn't want *to go stag* and begged me *to go in his place*. I gave her every excuse I could think of, but then she reminded me that I *owed her one*, so I *caved*.

Since Frank canceled *last minute*, I only had a half an hour to get ready. I squeezed Marie and told her we'd have to *take a rain check* for our chill time. She snorted in response as I gently set her down off of the couch. Minnie slowly opened her eyes, and then shut them tight again. I patted her on the head and told her not to wait up for me.

Irritated, I *threw off* my soft blanket and headed into my closet. Clothes were everywhere. I also didn't have time **to hang up** my laundry yesterday, so everything was **wrinkled**. First, I **tried on** some **slacks** with a new **peplum top** I had gotten on sale earlier that month. I was comfortable, but to be honest, the slacks did look a bit **frumpy,** even with my nude **heels**. Next, I tried on my pink silk **blouse**, and I **paired it with** my very uncomfortable, but cute, black **miniskirt**. Super sexy, but probably *a bit much* for a work event. Then I considered my cream **button down**. I put it on with my **tweed trousers**. I even slipped on my **loafers** thinking it would complete the look. I liked it, but it just didn't feel sophisticated enough. I switched **tops** thinking this would help. I tried a **dressy tank** with a **cardigan** instead. Still a no. I *ditched* the cardigan for a **blazer**, but that just looked too **stiff**. Annoyed, I kicked *off* my loafers, and *huffed and puffed a bit*. Marie took refuge in her bed, but she kept her eyes on me. I gave her a treat and asked if she wanted to go instead. She snorted and rolled over for a belly rub. A little calmer now, I started *to dig to the back of my closet,* in hopes of finding some spectacular garment that I had somehow forgotten about. To my surprise, I found my old graduation **dress**. I absolutely loved this dress! So **silky**, **flowy**, and most importantly, **flattering**- it was *the real deal*. I also loved the **print**. It was so **original,** and it **offset** the traditional **cut of** the dress. Thankfully it still zipped. I couldn't believe it wasn't **too tight**. I did a little dance in my closet. Marie wagged her tail. I still loved **getting dressed up**, even if I was exhausted.

I grabbed my favorite **scarf**, and **pumps**, and laid them by the door. I *dumped everything out of* my **tote bag** and got out the essentials to transfer into my **clutch** for the evening. Good to go, with 5 minutes to spare.

Let's Review

Clothing Vocabulary & Expressions

- *Comfy:* comfortable.
- *Baggy:* loose fitting.
- *To slip on:* to easily put on.
- *To hang up:* to place something on a hook or hanger.
- *To be wrinkled:* to have slight unwanted folds; not smooth.
- *Slacks:* casual trousers.
- *Peplum top:* cinches at the top of the waist, and has a ruffle flowing out and away from the body.
- *Frumpy:* unfashionable; out of date; shabby.
- *Blouse:* a loose shirt for women that is more dressy than a regular shirt.
- *To pair together:* to put things together temporarily.
- *Tweed trousers: trousers:* made with tightly woven wool.
- *Loafers:* a type of dress shoe that is easily slipped on or off without laces.
- *A bit much:* to be somewhat excessive or overbearing.
- *A tank:* a sleeveless top; also called a tank top.
- *A cardigan:* a knitted long sleeve sweater that opens in front and closes with buttons down the front.
- *To look stiff:* to look boring or too serious.
- *To offset:* to balance or compensate.
- *The cut of a garment:* the style or shape of a garment, not it's fabric or color.
- *Pumps:* similar to heels but shorter in height.
- *Tote bag:* a mid to large sized rectangular bag with two parallel handles.
- *Clutch:* a small flat purse without handles or straps.

Additional Verbs & Vocabulary

- *Grueling:* extremely tiring and exhausting.
- *To fling off:* to take off in a quick and careless way.
- *To veg out:* to spend time idly or passively.
- *To deal with it:* to take the necessary action to solve a problem.
- *To be as snug as a bug:* very cozy and comfortable.
- *To drift off to sleep:* to gradually go to sleep.
- *To come down with:* to contract and develop a sickness.
- *To go stag:* to go to an event by oneself.
- *To owe someone one:* to be indebted to someone because of a favor they did for you.
- *To cave:* to surrender to the wants of someone else.
- *Last minute:* the latest possible time before an event.
- *To take a rain check:* to accept a postponement.
- *To ditch:* to get rid of something.
- *To huff and puff:* to breathe in a loud or heavy way in response to physical limitations, frustration, annoyance, or stress.
- *To dump out:* to empty the contents of a container or bag, by turning it upside down and shaking it out.

HAPPILY MARRIED.

Brian and Elizabeth had met years ago at the town fair. Right away, Brian was **taken with** Elizabeth's beauty. Elizabeth, on the other hand, didn't give Brian much thought. She had just gotten out of a terrible long distance relationship and wasn't looking for anything new at the moment. Not to mention that while Brian was very clever and tenderhearted, he was also rather shy. Even though he felt *drawn to* Elizabeth, he simply couldn't *muster up* the courage to approach her.

Years later, Elizabeth began **seeing someone** new, David. David seemed like a dream. He was handsome, very charming, smart, and *down to earth*. He and Elizabeth had so much in common, and shared similar interests such as poetry, traveling, and nature. In fact, their very first date was a nature hike. They **hit it off** almost instantly. Elizabeth quickly began to **fall for** David. Just the sight of him gave her **butterflies in her stomach**. He was such a great catch, and she was absolutely **smitten** with him.

The couple had been **going out** for a few months. Everything seemed so easy. One morning while out with her friends, Elizabeth's phone rang. It was David. Her jaw dropped as she heard him say the dreaded phrase "***We need to talk.***" Elizabeth was devastated. She knew what was coming. As expected, over dinner that evening, David **ended things** with Elizabeth. He felt that they had been **drifting apart** for some time now and needed to **move on**.

Months passed, and it was suddenly fall. There was a crisp chill to the air, and the leaves had begun changing colors. It was

Elizabeth's favorite time of the year. This particular morning, she was downtown for a meeting. When she was younger, Elizabeth was enchanted by the city. The enormous skyscrapers, *the hustle and bustle* of everyday life, the constant changing of the city- it was all very magical to her. However, as of late, she had been feeling rather disenchanted by the city and with life in general. She felt somewhat lost in her career, not to mention her personal life.

Elizabeth checked her watch. The meeting had ended surprisingly early, and she found herself with some *time on her hands. Being that* she was already downtown, she decided to *round the corner*, and pop into her favorite bookshop on tenth street.

Entering the shop, Elizabeth took a deep breath, pulled her hair back into a low bun, and dug her glasses out of her purse. She was *browsing* the new poets' section when she heard a familiar voice from the other side of the bookshelf. She peeked through the books to see none other than quiet, unassuming Brian Adams. She *gazed* a bit too long deciding whether to approach him, because while taking a gulp of his coffee, Brain **caught her eye**. Surprised, he choked and *spilled* his scalding cappuccino all down his blue and white polka dotted shirt. Elizabeth *giggled* and rushed over with some tissues from her bag. They both had a good laugh and began to catch up on everything from Brain's latest trip to Egypt, to Elizabeth's new cat, Biscuits.

The next morning, Brian gave Elizabeth a call. This time, he didn't need to muster up any courage, he immediately **asked her out** to dinner. The rest is history. Eventually the two **got hitched, settled down**, and had a family of their own. Brian and Elizabeth have four grown children and eight grandchildren. They have been happily married for 40 years.

Let's Review

Love Expressions

• *To be taken with someone*: to find someone attractive or interesting.
• *To be drawn to:* to be attracted to someone or something.
• *To see someone:* to be dating someone.
• *To hit it off with someone:* to get along well with someone.
• *To fall for someone:* to begin to love someone.
• *To be a great catch:* someone who has all the great qualities that make a great romantic partner.
• *To have butterflies in one's stomach:* a nervous feeling in one's stomach.
• *To be smitten with someone:* to be infatuated or in love with someone.
• *We need to talk:* a well-known phrase that signifies the process of ending a relationship.
• *To end things with someone:* to sever a relationship or to break up.
• *To drift apart:* to gradually lose interest in or affection for each other.
• *To move on:* to accept that something has changed, to let it go, and begin something new.
• *To catch someone's eye:* to get someone's attention by making eye contact.
• *To ask someone out:* to invite someone out to dinner or another social event, as a way of starting a romantic relationship.
• *To get hitched:* to get married.
• *To settle down:* to begin to live a quiet and steady life.

Extra Vocabulary & Verbs

- *To muster up:* to rouse or gather up emotions or abilities.
- *To be down to earth:* to be unpretentious; humble; genuine.
- *Hustle and bustle:* a large amount of work in a busy and noisy environment.
- *To have time on one's hands:* to have free or extra time.
- *Being that:* since; because.
- *To pop into:* to visit briefly; occasionally unannounced.
- *To browse:* to look casually.
- *To gaze:* to stare, usually in admiration.
- *To spill:* to cause or allow something to flow out of a container.
- *To giggle:* a small, quiet laugh; usually when one is nervous about something.

FRIENDS.

After about an hour, Peter politely **ducked out** of the meeting, to phone his buddy Andrew. The speaker had been **droning on and on** about topics that were completely meaningless. Andrew was traveling for work and put Peter's call on speakerphone while driving. Peter reported to Andrew that the big meeting was **for the birds**, and then asked him if he could meet in a half an hour for lunch. Andrew said he was **hungry as a horse** and would definitely meet Peter.

The two friends met a little later at their favorite pizzeria. Andrew **wolfed down** some fries as an appetizer before the two could even have a chance to chat. Finally, Andrew asked how Peter's new job was going. Peter revealed that he wasn't really enjoying it. He talked about his new colleagues and the difficulty he was having *fitting into* his new environment. He talked about his new desk mate Earl who was not only a massive *kiss up*, but an even bigger **eager beaver**. He also told Andrew about the new boss who **went ape** anytime anyone missed a deadline. He also described the office secretary who *talks everyone's ears off*, and who, not surprisingly, **let the cat out of the bag** about an upcoming pay cut next month. Peter elaborated by saying that he really regretted switching companies. Andrew agreed saying *"curiosity killed the cat."*

After finishing up their pizzas, Andrew asked if Peter wanted to grab a coffee before heading back to work. At the coffee shop, Peter asked about Andrew's cousin who had been staying with him for the last month. Andrew tried to be delicate, but eventually admitted that his cousin seemed to be **leeching off** him. Not only that, but he unapologetically **hogged** their shared computer. He also told Peter that his younger cousin was very active, and into exercise. Andrew stressed that he himself wasn't a **spring chicken** anymore and really missed being able to relax at home. He was quite the **bookworm** and missed curing up with a good book in the evenings without being *bothered* to exercise.

As the friends got up to leave the coffee shop, Andrew asked Peter if he was going to have his usual post coffee smoke. Peter proudly informed Andrew that he had finally quit smoking. He had stopped **cold turkey** just last week and was doing very well. Andrew threw his arms around his friend and congratulated him on a job well done! He knew how much Peter had struggled with smoking all his adult life. The two friends parted ways and made it through the rest of their day encouraged, and grateful for their friendship.

Let's Review

Animal Phrasal Verbs & Expressions

• *To duck out:* to leave suddenly, sometimes without notifying others.
• *To drone on and on:* to speak about something for a long time in a monotone boring voice.
• *For the birds:* useless; ridiculous; foolish.
• *As hungry as a horse:* very hungry.
• *To wolf down:* to eat something quickly and ravenously.
• *To be an eager beaver:* to be alert, energetic, and zealous.
• *To go ape:* to become uncontrollably angry.
• *To let the cat out of the bag:* to tell a secret.
• *Curiosity killed the cat:* being too curious can cause trouble.
• *To leech off:* to get things from others without earning or deserving them.
• *To hog:* to selfishly keep all of something for oneself.
• *To be a spring chicken:* to be young.
• *To be a bookworm:* a person who loves and is devoted to books.
• *To go cold turkey:* to stop a habit instantly.

Additional Expressions

• *To be a kiss up:* someone who uses flattery or pleasing behavior to manipulate someone into doing something for them.
• *To talk everyone's ears off:* to talk for a very long time.
• *To heading back:* to return to a place one has been to before, or the place from which one came.
• *To be bothered to do something:* to have a burden of doing something.

❖ ❖ ❖

PRACTICAL AMERICAN ENGLISH

THE VISIT.

My parents will be visiting me this weekend, and I have so many things to do before they arrive in the morning. It has been a long day at work, and I would love to just **plop down** on the couch and **flip through** the channels. Unfortunately, duty calls.

I start by **putting away** all my laundry. As I'm **hanging up** my clothes, I am reminded that I really need to **go through** my clothes. I go ahead and **yank down** a couple pairs of jeans that are absolutely too tight, as well as a few dresses that I'm busting out of, and **throw** them in a bag. I'll send these with my parents as hand-me-downs for my youngest sister.

After all the clean laundry is put away, I start a new load. While the clothes are in the wash, I fluff the ones that have been sitting in the dryer all week. Then, I **pick up** and organize while the clothes are **washing** and **fluffing**. All my furniture is solid wood, and unfortunately gets incredibly dusty. I dust everything, and begin to clean the windows, when I hear my dog Marie scratching at the back door to go out. I let her out and **scrounge around** for a snack while I'm waiting for her to come back inside. I *scarf down* some chips, and I hear the washer **shut off**, so I go and **switch the laundry**. I take the fluffed towels into the living room and let Marie back inside. She races into the living room and **curls up** on top of the enormous pile of warm towels.

Now I'll attack the bathrooms. I spray everything down, and then scrub the toilets. Next, I clean the shower and the tub. As I'm **wiping down** the bathroom sinks and countertops, I notice that one of the soap dispensers is leaking and has spilled down onto the floor. I quickly **wipe it all up,** and rinse and **wring out** my rag.

I decide to take a break and make some dinner. I **run** some water into a pot and put it on to boil. I'll just have a simple pasta and some veggies. I check to see if I have any garlic because what's pasta without garlic? I find 2 cloves of garlic, 1 zucchini, and some tomatoes I had pulled off the vine yesterday after work. While I wait on the water to boil, I **sip on** my coffee and look out the window. It's such a lovely day. I **crack the windows open** to let a bit of fresh air flow inside. I hear Mr. Dilly's lawnmower roaring next door, and Rex barking across the street. I wonder if the Nelson's are back from Jamaica yet. I remember that I need to return her pie dish.

I **shuffle** back to the kitchen, daydreaming about Jamaica, and I **trip** over Marie's rope. I fall flat on my face, and spill my coffee all over my brand new rug. I try not to panic, grab a dish towel, and begin to **sop** up as much coffee as I can before spraying the cleaner and scrubbing it to death.

After what seemed like an eternity, I finally get the stain out of the rug, and make my dinner. I'm beat! I **rear back** in my favorite velvet chair in front of the T.V. **to chill**. Marie hops up onto the back of the couch across from me. As usual, she *stares a hole in me* while I eat. While she's not getting any of my pasta, I decide maybe we could use some ice cream for dessert.

The ice cream shop is just up the street, so I ask Marie if she wants to join me. I **hook her up** and **head out** the front door. The rest of the cleaning will have to wait until we get back.

Let's Review

Home Expressions, Vocabulary & Verbs

- *To plop down:* to sit or lie down in a heavy and careless way.
- *To flip through:* to keep changing the channel on TV channels quickly in order to check what shows are on.
- *To put away:* to return something to its proper place.
- *To go through:* to examine a collection of things carefully to organize it.
- *To yank down:* to forcefully pull or remove something.
- *Hand-me-downs:* used garments passed from one person to another.
- *To fluff the clothes:* to reheat clean clothes in a dryer in order to remove wrinkles.
- *To pick up the house:* to tidy it.
- *To scrounge around:* to look in various places to find something one needs.
- *To scarf down:* to eat very quickly.
- *To shut off:* to remove electronic power from a device or machine.
- *To switch the laundry:* to move the wet clothes from the washer to the dryer.
- *To curl up:* to lie down or sit with one's arms and legs bent close to the body.
- *To wipe down:* to clean the surface of something.
- *To wipe up:* to remove a substance, usually liquid, with a cloth.
- *To wring out:* to remove excess water.
- *To run water:* to turn a faucet and allow the water to flow out.
- *To sip:* to take small drinks.
- *To crack open:* to open slightly.

- *To shuffle:* to move by dragging or sliding one's feet- not lifting.
- *To trip:* to stumble over something and lose one's balance.
- *To sop:* to absorb a liquid.
- *To be eat:* to be exhausted.
- *To rear back:* to lean back.
- *To chill:* to relax.
- *To stare a hole in someone:* to stare at someone unapologetically and intensely.
- *To hook up an animal:* to attach the animal's collar to a leash.

BLUE BRIDGES.

On Saturdays, Martin and Eddie like to spend the morning at their favorite park- Blue Bridges. It's only **a stone's throw's away** from their downtown bungalow- right off High Street. So, after a toasted almond bagel for Martin and some eggs for Eddie, they **take off** on foot to Blue Bridges. Eddie leads the way, sniffing every **nook and cranny,** and barking from time to time at the delivery men they pass along the way.

Eddie is so eager to get to the park, that he basically **drags** Martin down High Street. Martin doesn't mind until in his haste, Eddie causes Martin to **slam into** a lamp post just outside the entrance of the park. Martin is a bit **shook up**, but **stumbles** on into the park nonetheless. He can't wait for Martin to **let him loose**. His favorite spot is just past the infamous Blue Bridge. There is a large open green area where he likes to run off his leash. Martin never has to worry about Eddie **darting off** or disappearing. The two are inseparable- like **two peas in a pod**.

Finally, they cross the bridge. Martin unhooks Eddie, and **chucks** his favorite stick about half way to the pond. While Eddie chases the stick, Martin **stoops down** to **pick** a few daises for their neighbor Gail. Eddie comes racing back, leaping over puddles, and **ripping through** the tall grasses. He proudly drops the stick at Martin's feet. Impatiently, Eddie **twirls** and **yips**, as he waits for Martin to **hurl** his stick again across the park. Eddie **takes off** before Martin even releases his throw.

Martin follows Eddie at a much slower pace. He **tromps** through the tall grasses, and **hops** over a few small puddles. Eddie is

taking his time returning to Martin and is most assuredly spying on the frogs down at the edge of the pond. Martin decides to wander around a bit and decompress after a difficult work week. Out of the corner of his eye he sees some daffodils. Gail had just planted daffodils in her front yard last Tuesday. They really were quite soothing, and so happy, *"Just like Gail,"* he thought. Martin wondered what Gail was up to this morning. He didn't see her yesterday, and was wondering if she found her purple scarf she had told him about. She was so upset about it. Martin is so caught up in his thoughts, that he accidently **bumps into** the big Maple right before the pond. Martin is *caught off guard*, but otherwise fine. He **dusts** himself **off** and decides to climb up to his favorite branch for a bit before meeting up with Eddie.

Martin **straddles** the branch, **dangling** his feet in the air. He can see Eddie up ahead **sneaking up on** the frogs and rolling on his stick. Martin enjoys a few more minutes in the tree before **jumping down** and **scooping up** his freshly picked flowers. He smiles thinking about surprising Gail with the daisies.

Let's Review

Outdoor Vocabulary Expressions, & Verbs

- *A stone's throw's away:* a short distance.
- *To take off on foot:* to begin an excursion by walking.
- *Nook and cranny:* every part of a place.
- *To drag:* to move by pulling or sliding across a surface.
- *To slam into:* to forcefully crash into something.
- *To be shook up:* to be emotionally or physically upset.
- *To stumble:* to lose one's balance and almost fall.
- *To let something loose:* to allow something to move freely.
- *To dart off:* to move away quickly and suddenly.
- *Like two peas in a pod:* to be very similar.
- *To chuck/ to hurl:* to throw something with great force.
- *To stoop down*: to bend over and down.
- *To pick flowers: t*o break the stem of a flower and collect it.
- *To rip through:* to move powerfully through something.
- *To twirl:* to quickly spin or revolve.
- *To yip*: a short sharp cry or bark of an animal.
- *To take off:* to depart.
- *To tromp:* to walk heavily.
- *To hop:* to move by jumping.
- *To take one's time:* to not hurry or rush.
- *To bump into:* to accidentally walk into something or someone.
- *To dust off:* to clean from dust, dirt, or other small particles.
- *To straddle:* to sit, stand, or walk with one's legs wide apart.
- *To dangle:* to hang or swing loosely.
- *To sneak up on:* to quietly get near to someone without being seen

or heard, usually in order to surprise or scare someone.

• *To scoop up:* to quickly lift something or someone up with one's arms and hands.

MILO & MAX.

"I can't believe I have to **fork out** $600 **bucks** for a new tire," thought Milo. The car was fairly new, making Milo even more upset to have to **run up** his credit card **to cover** the bill. He prefers to pay cash for everything **up front** in full.

Milo doesn't enjoy spending money. Some might even call him a bit of a **penny pincher**. His brother Max certainly would. Milo is so focused on his finances that he rarely will spend the money to eat out with Jim, or even catch a movie. He always says he would rather *save his money for a rainy day*.

This of course *bores his brother Max to tears*. Max is the exact opposite of his brother Milo. As soon as he gets some **cash**, **it burns a hole in his pocket**. He enjoys trying new restaurants in the city, traveling, and visiting his many friends across the USA. He has many hobbies and **lives paycheck to paycheck** to enjoy them all. His carefree lifestyle got him into trouble a few times, **maxing out** his credit card on adventurous trips. Thankfully Milo *bailed him out* by loaning him the money, but now Max **owes him a pretty penny**.

On the flip side, Milo **doesn't owe anyone a dime**. In high school, he worked 2 jobs to save up for college, and he graduated college with zero debt. Not only was he debt free, but in college he was able to save up even more money for a down payment on his first house his junior year of college. This year, he paid off his house, sold his old *two door*, and bought his new car in cash.

While he has focused on saving his money over the years, no one would dare call Milo **stingy**. He may not like to spend his money on himself, but he is no **cheapskate** when it comes to helping others. He is very generous towards others. Just last week, Milo *found out* that his neighbors couldn't afford to send their son Sam on the class trip to Boston. That very night, he called and insisted on paying for Sam's trip. He loves to help others who are **down and out**, or just a little **strapped for cash**.

Let's Review

Money Expressions, Vocabulary, & Verbs

- *To fork out:* to spend a large amount of money on something, out of necessity not desire.
- *Bucks:* dollars.
- *To run up:* to use a lot of something; to borrow a lot of money.
- *To cover the bill:* to pay for the bill.
- *Cash:* money in coins or bills; legal tender.
- *To pay up front:* to pay in advance.
- *A penny pincher:* someone who doesn't like to spend their money.
- *To save for a rainy day:* to save money for a future time when it might be needed unexpectantly.
- *To burn a hole in one's pocket:* to be very eager to spend one's money.
- *To live paycheck to paycheck:* to spend all of one's paycheck on living expenses, without any extra left over.
- *To max out one's credit card:* to use all the available credit.
- *To owe someone a pretty penny:* to owe someone a lot of money.
- *On the flip side:* another way to say, *on the other hand*.
- *To not owe anyone a dime:* to owe nothing to no one.
- *To be stingy:* unwilling to share with others.
- *Cheapskate:* someone who is stingy.
- *To be down and out:* to be very poor and without hope of improving one's situation.
- *To be strapped for cash:* to be in need of money.

Additional Expressions & Vocabulary

- *To be bored to tears:* to be so extremely bored, that one wants to cry in frustration.
- *To find out:* to discover.
- *To bail someone out:* to help someone out of a difficult situation.
- *Two door:* a car with only two doors.

ABOUT THE AUTHOR

Jessica Smith

Jessica discovered her love of languages and cultures over a decade ago while living in Italy with her husband as missionaries. She understands firsthand what it means to live as a foreigner, and to learn a language from scratch. Jessica is TESOL certified, and has 13 years experience teaching ESL. This is her first book.

Jessica currently lives in North Carolina with her husband Eric, her children, and her doxies Marie and Minnie. Jessica has many other passions including art, travel, and her faith in Jesus.

Find out more @jessicateachesenglish on Instagram.

Made in the USA
Las Vegas, NV
17 November 2023